Highlights PUZZLEMANIA®

Wyatt's TRY-ITS

Having trouble finding sports in "Go for the Gold!" on pages 22–23? Placing a ruler along a line of letters makes it easier to see the words—especially those tricky diagonal ones!

Highlightskids.com

Check out the Highlights Kids website. It's awesome! You'll find tons more mind-bending puzzles, great games, and loads of jokes and riddles. And that's just the tip of the iceberg. There are also stories, articles, crafts, and much more. It's 100 percent Wyatt-approved!

Look Again!

Can you find jigsaw pieces hidden on the cover?

Answer on page 30

Cover illustrated by Dave Clegg

Yo, Puzzlemaniacs!

Wyatt the Riot™ here, there, and everywhere! Are you a pizza fan? This book is like a puzzle pizza with the works! So sharpen your appetite—and your pencil—and grab a slice!

Don't forget to check out my blog. That's the sticker story on page 24. Find out what happens when Max and I try the ⊙ toss game at the county fair.

And be sure to take a look at my personal puzzle pick: "Half-Pipe Hilarity" on page 6. Man, I'd love to skate *that* park!

Over & out!

Wyatt

Half-Pipe Hilarity

Roll on in! There are some strange sights at the skate park today. Can you find at least 25 odd, weird, or wacky things in this picture?

Find Your Favorites

Olivia has made a list of puzzles for you—as usual!

Illustrated by Mike Dammer

Pitcher Perfect

This game is heating up. While the teams battle it out, see if you can keep your cool and find at least 20 differences between these pictures.

Answer on page 30

Illustrated by Daryll Collins

Rock It

These rock climbers got their ropes tangled. Can you set them straight? Follow each rope from the climber on the mountain to find out who his or her partner is.

Answer on page 30

4

What's Bugging You?

When Molly sat down in the cafeteria, there was a **spider on the table**! Lots of people had something to say about it. Unscramble each word in capital letters to see what each person told her.

Answer on page 31

1. The **cafeteria worker** asked, "Would it like a burger and SEFLI?"
   <u>F L I E S</u>

2. The **English teacher** said, "May I have a DROW with it?"
   — — — —

3. The **principal** said, "No STEP allowed at school!"
   — — — —

4. The **secretary** said, "I've never seen this YPET before."
   — — — —

5. The **monitor** said, "No creeping down the LAHL!"
   — — — —

6. The **school bus driver** said, "Don't let it go for a NIPS."
   — — — —

7. The **swim coach** said, "Let's see if it can do the WALCR."
   — — — — —

8. The **computer teacher** said, "I'll see if it has its own BEW TIES."
   — — — — — — —

9. The **music teacher** said, "Don't let the itsy bitsy critter go up the TROUTWASPE."
   — — — — — — — — — —

10. The **math teacher** said, "Catch it quick, before it PLUMTILSIES!"
    — — — — — — — — — —

Illustrated by Kelly Kennedy   Puzzle by Jacqueline Horsfall

5

Half-Pipe Hilarity

Roll on in! There are some strange sights at the skate park today. Can you find at least **25** odd, weird, or wacky things in this picture?

Illustrated by Garry Colby

Nice to See You!

Hi! We're glad you stopped by. We've hidden **22** ways to say *hello* in this grid. Look up, down, across, backwards, and diagonally to greet as many as you can.

Answer on page 30

Word List

AHOY
BONJOUR
BUENOS DIAS
GOOD DAY
GOOD MORNING
GOOD TO SEE YOU
GREETINGS
GUTEN TAG
HELLO
HEY
HI THERE
HIYA
HOLA
HOW ARE YOU?
HOW DO YOU DO?
HOWDY
JAMBO
KONICHIWA
QUE PASA?
SALUTATIONS
WHAT'S UP?
WIE GEHTS?

```
Y J A M B O M V G H T H B Y
B A W I H C I N O K E Y Y P
O K G H B O N J O U R Y E H
D C N I Y H O W D Y D H S O
U G I T E W H A T S U P N W
O U N H H E X H O S G J O A
Y T R E D O H I S E R W I R
O E O R B E L Y E E E I T E
D N M E L Y L A E Y E E A Y
W T D L A T E R Y A T G T O
O A O Y A D D O O G I E U U
H G O B Y E H U U H N H L E
L R G A S A P E U Q G T A Y
B U E N O S D I A S S S S B
```

Add a Letter

You can use the letter **A** to turn a pencil into a pelican. Take **PENCIL** and add an **A**. Move the letters around to make **PELICAN**. Use your stickers finish the job. Then see if you can figure out the rest.

Answer on page 30

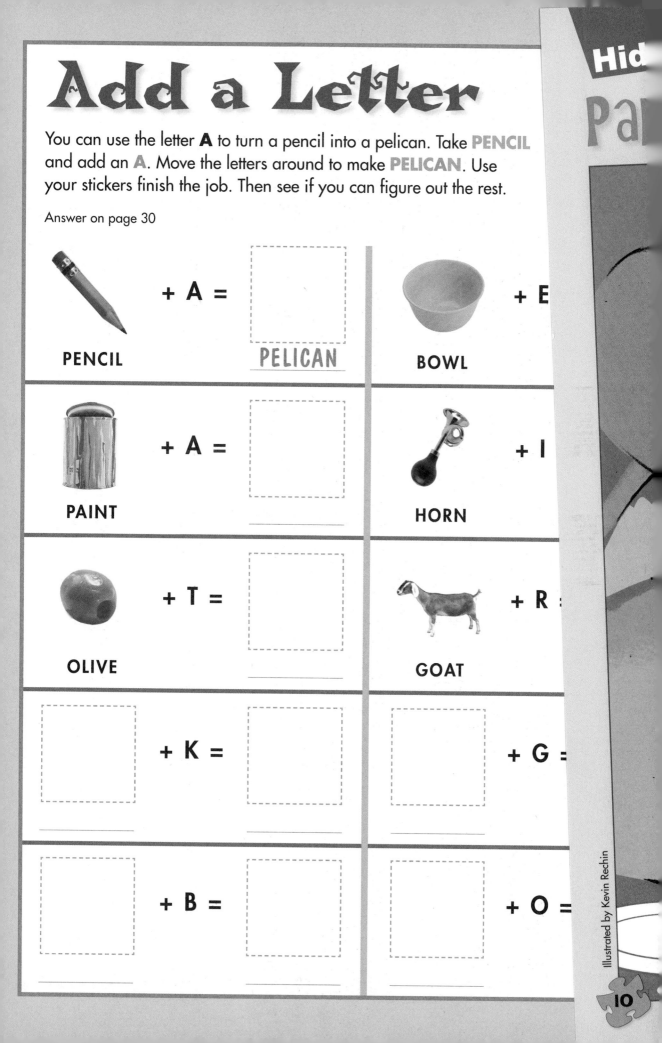

PENCIL   + **A** =   PELICAN

BOWL   + E

PAINT   + **A** =

HORN   + I

OLIVE   + **T** =

GOAT   + R

+ **K** =

+ **G** =

+ **B** =

+ **O** =

Illustrated by Kevin Rechin

rty Favors

There is more than meets the eye at this birthday party. Can you find the hidden objects?

Answer on page 31

toy car

sailboat

ruler

comb

spoon

snake

banana

megaphone

paintbrush

trowel

book

envelope

toothbrush

mitten

teapot

feather

pencil

paperclip

spatula

carrot

fish

fishhook

slice of pizza

Stop, Look, and List

Are you ready for a trivia challenge? Fill in each box with a name or word. It must begin with the letter at the top of the column. We put in a few of our favorites to get you started.

Answer on page 31

CATEGORY	S	T	O	P
Zoo animals				
Kitchen objects				
Words with **TT** in Them			otter	
Art Words	sculpture			
Pets' names				Princess
School words			organizer	
Silly salad ingredients		toasted tennis shoes		
Shapes				

Math Mirth

The Math Club is holding its annual comedy night. Can you guess the answers to these riddles? All the letters you need are in the word list. Each fraction tells you which letters to use.

Answer on page 31

1. What do math teachers eat?

___ ___ ___ ___ ___ ___ ___ ___

___ ___ ___ ___

First ½ of **SQUASH**
First ⅓ of **ARTIST**
Last ½ of **POEM**
Last ½ of **CONCEALS**

2. Why did the math teacher stop singing karaoke?

___ ___ ___ ___ ___ ___ ___ ___

___ ___ ___ ___ ___.

Last ⅗ of **USHER**
Middle ⅓ of **MANUAL**
Last ½ of **CUCUMBER**
Middle ⅓ of **BEWARE**
First ⅓ of **SUPERSTAR**

Illustrated by Mike Moran

Best of the Bunch

Ari is trying to pick the perfect balloon for her best friend's birthday. You can help her by finding all the matching balloons. There are 18 pairs that are exactly alike. When you've found them all, one balloon will be left. That's the one for Ari. Can you find it?

Answer on page 31

Look Sharp!

We have something to show you! First, use your stickers to finish the picture. Then take a closer look. There are at least 30 things that begin with the letters **SH**. How many can you find? Sharpen your pencil and you should begin.

Answer on page 31

Illustrated by Tim Haggerty

Moo-ve It Along

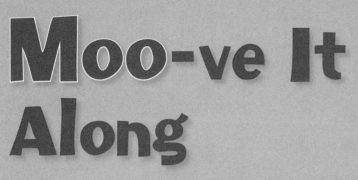

These five cows have wandered away from their owners. Using the clues below, can you figure out which cow belongs to which rancher?

Answer on page 31

Moosic

Cowly

Munch

Cuddles

Ferdie

Use the chart to keep track of your answers. Put an **X** in each box that can't be true and an **O** in boxes that match.

	Moosic	Munch	Cowly	Cuddles	Ferdie
Buck					
Jeannie					
Roy					
Sasha					
Tex					

1. Buck's cow is two colors.
2. Jeannie and her cow have the same number of letters in their names.
3. Tex is not fond of longhorns, but he likes bells.
4. Sasha's cow, which does not have horns, is the same color as another cow, but not the same color as Buck's cow.

18

Illustrated by Dave Clegg   Puzzle by Lori Mortensen

Fruit Salad

Each of these grids holds one type of fruit. Fill in the boxes so that each row, column, and 6-letter section contains the letters of that fruit. We've filled in some of the letters to get you started. Can you fill in the rest?

A

G	R	A	P	E	S
	P	E		A	G
	G		A		
	A				E
A	S			R	
		P	G	S	A

B

O	R	A	N	G	E
E		G			
			R		G
R			A		
N	E	O		R	
G	A		E		O

C

Q	U	I	N	C	E
C				N	C
	N	U	I	Q	
		C		U	
	I			N	I
I	Q	C		E	

19

Pizza Q's

Answers on page 32

Puzzles by Carly Schuna

Illustrated by Mike Moran

Delivery Dilemma

Can you help Pete get the pizza delivered while it's still hot?

Start

Finish

One of Everything!

What would you put on your dream pizza? Design your fantasy pizza here!

Pizza Quiz

Can you guess which statements are true and which are false?

a. Chicago-style pizza is famous for its spicy sauce.

T or F

b. A Stromboli is like a rolled up pizza pocket.

T or F

c. The largest pizza ever baked measured 122 feet across.

T or F

d. More ricotta goes on pizza than any other cheese.

T or F

Odd Slice Out

One of these slices is different from the others. Can you tell which one it is?

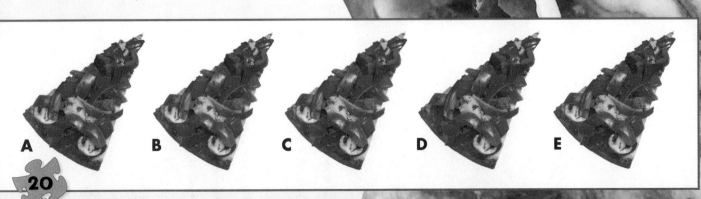

A   B   C   D   E

Old World Pizza

Neapolitan is the original type of pizza that was first made in Italy. Can you make at least twenty words from the letters in NEAPOLITAN?

_____ _____
_____ _____
_____ _____
_____ _____
_____ _____
_____ _____
_____ _____
_____ _____
_____ _____
_____ _____

Mixed-Up Orders

Peyton, Isaac, and Ethan ordered three types of pizza: Hawaiian, pepperoni, and cheese. Who ordered which kind?

1. Ethan had pineapple on his pizza.

2. Peyton is a vegetarian.

Go for the Gold!

Twenty-six Summer Olympic sports are hiding in this grid. Look for them up, down, across, backwards, and diagonally. Be a good sport and find as many as you can.

Answer on page 32

Word List

- ~~ARCHERY~~
- BADMINTON
- BASKETBALL
- BEACH VOLLEYBALL
- BIATHLON
- CANOEING
- CYCLING
- DECATHLON
- DISCUS
- DIVING
- FENCING
- GYMNASTICS
- HANDBALL
- HIGH JUMP
- JUDO
- LONG JUMP
- MARATHON
- PENTATHLON
- SAILING
- SHOTPUT
- SOCCER
- SPRINTING
- SWIMMING
- TENNIS
- TRIATHLON
- WRESTLING

```
J B L B G H B B O B S L E D V
K N L H W R E S T L I N G E D
O B A F I Q A R E C C O S X D
N A B G N G C A N O E I N G I
E D T N H Y H A N D B A L L V
G M E I Q M V J T E N N I S I
N I K M P N O F U O Q U J U N
I N S M M A L M O M T O T C G
T T A I U S L A F O P R O S S
N O B W J T E R I E I A X I N
I N L S G I Y A N A H G Y D O
R V U G N C B T T T O Y R E W
P F G J O S A H I M C S E C B
S E E I L T L O S K K H H A O
A N Q J H O L N D C E O C T A
I C U L N A Q O A U Y T R H R
L I O C Y C L I N G J P A L D
I N C S P O R T S G I U M O I
N G N N O L H T A I B T O N N
G F I G U R E S K A T I N G G
```

BONUS PUZZLE
We've also hidden five Winter Olympic sports in the grid. Can you find them?

Illustrated by Wendy Wax

23

Wyatt's dad helped him set up a blog that friends like you can read. Wyatt shares the news. Then you add stickers to the spaces to turn his blog into a funny story.

Profile

Wyatt Rogers

Friends

Ike Howard

Anna Shaw

Max Patel

Lucas Vega

Jake Rogers

Olivia Rogers

Comments

You guys went hog wild at the fair. ☺

Isabel Vega

Fair Game

The county fair opened today! I went with Max, Olivia, and

my parents. Right away, Olivia dragged Mom off to see

which 4-H animals had won a blue   STICKER   . Max and I

wanted to try the roller   STICKER   , so Dad went with us. There

was a long   STICKER   , but the ride was awesome! After that we

all rode the Octopus, the Twister, and the Screaming   STICKER   .

   Dad's   STICKER   looked kind of pale. "How about taking

a break?" he asked.

   Max and I were hungry, so we each had a hot dog with

spicy   STICKER   . For some reason, Dad passed.

   "I'll just sit under this   STICKER   awhile," he said. Then

he gave us tickets to play the carnival games.

24

We tried bowling, sticky darts, and the dunking   STICKER   . It was fun, but

neither of us won a   STICKER   . We were down to one ticket apiece when

we got to the ring toss. The game cost two. "Go for it, Max," I said, and

we each handed the   STICKER   operator a ticket.

Every ring Max threw landed perfectly! He won the grand   STICKER   : a big

stuffed pink pig. I cracked up—till he said that since it was half mine, I would have to

carry it half the time. Talk about embarrassing!

Good thing we ran into Mom and Olivia

at the Ferris   STICKER   .

Even better, Olivia loved the pig.

Over and out!

Wyatt

Illustrated by Mike Dammer

25

Vroom, Vroom!

Hugh is trying to catch up with his friends at the end of the trail. Can you find the one path that will lead him there? Once you've reached FINISH, write the letters you find along the way in the spaces below to answer the riddle.

Answer on page 32

Start

Illustrated by Ron Zalme

26

How do dogs like to travel?

___ ___   ___ ___ ___ ___ ___ - ___ - ___ ___ ___

Crisscross the U.S.A.

We've scoured the country and found **25** landmarks to place in this puzzle. They can fit in the grid just one way. Use the number of letters in each name to figure out where it belongs. Write in each landmark and cross it off the list as you go. Happy travels!

Answer on page 32

6 Letters
BIG SUR
COLOMA
DENALI

8 Letters
THE ALAMO
ALCATRAZ
BIG BASIN
FORT KNOX
HALF DOME
SALT LAKE
WIND CAVE

9 Letters
HOOVER DAM
MESA VERDE
PIKES PEAK

10 Letters
DELTA QUEEN
WHITE HOUSE

11 Letters
DEATH VALLEY
GRAND CANYON
MOUNT VERNON
SPACE NEEDLE

12 Letters
FALLINGWATER
HEARST CASTLE
NIAGARA FALLS
PLYMOUTH ROCK

14 Letters
~~BROOKLYN BRIDGE~~

15 Letters
STATUE OF LIBERTY

B R O O K L Y N B R I D G E

BONUS PUZZLE

Have you filled in all the words? Now write the shaded letters, in order from left to right and top to bottom, in the spaces below to answer this question.

What U.S. attraction is all it's cracked up to be?

___ ___ ___ ___   ___ ___ ___ ___ ___ ___ ___   ___ ___   ___ ___ ___ ___ ___

ANSWERS

Front Cover
Look Again!

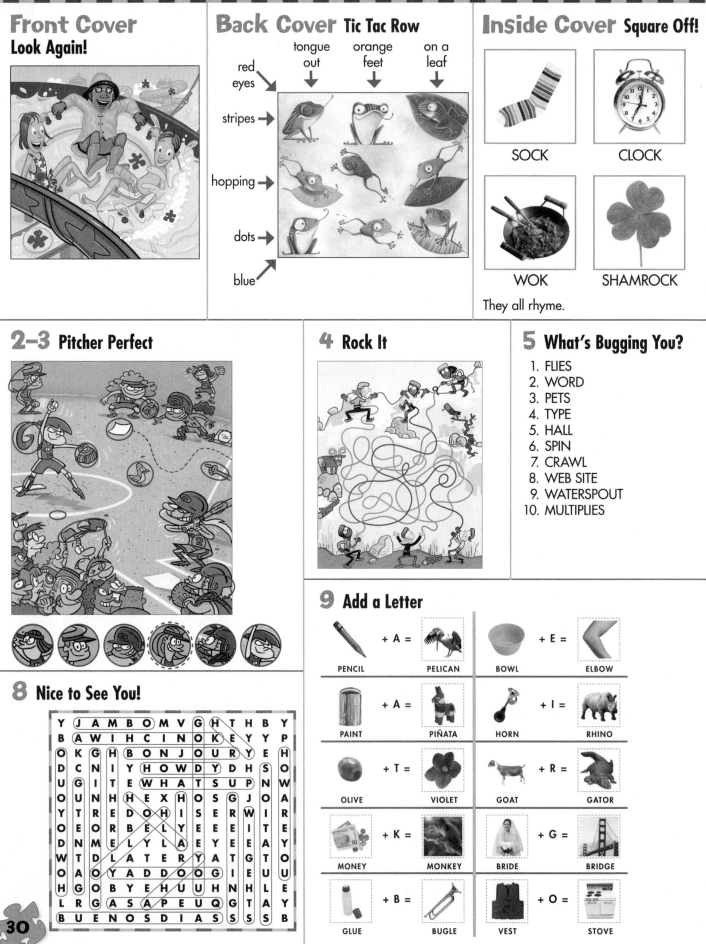

Back Cover — Tic Tac Row

tongue out — orange feet — on a leaf
red eyes
stripes
hopping
dots
blue

Inside Cover — Square Off!

SOCK — CLOCK
WOK — SHAMROCK

They all rhyme.

2–3 Pitcher Perfect

4 Rock It

5 What's Bugging You?

1. FLIES
2. WORD
3. PETS
4. TYPE
5. HALL
6. SPIN
7. CRAWL
8. WEB SITE
9. WATERSPOUT
10. MULTIPLIES

8 Nice to See You!

9 Add a Letter

PENCIL + A = PELICAN
BOWL + E = ELBOW
PAINT + A = PIÑATA
HORN + I = RHINO
OLIVE + T = VIOLET
GOAT + R = GATOR
MONEY + K = MONKEY
BRIDE + G = BRIDGE
GLUE + B = BUGLE
VEST + O = STOVE

30

10–11 Party Favors

12 Stop, Look, and List

Here are some possible answers. You may have thought of others.

Zoo animals – snake, tiger, orangutan, panda

Kitchen objects – spoon, toaster, oven, pan

Words with "TT" in them – settle, tattle, otter, pretty

Art words – sculpture, tracing paper, oil paints, portrait

Pets' names – Sparky, Torpedo, Oscar, Princess

School words – study, test, organizer, pencil

Silly salad ingredients – scrambled sardines, toasted tennis shoes, oatmeal, pan-fried peppermint

Shapes – square, triangle, octagon, pentagon

13 Math Mirth

What do math teachers eat?
SQUARE MEALS

Why did the math teacher stop singing karaoke?
HER NUMBER WAS UP.

14–15 Best of the Bunch

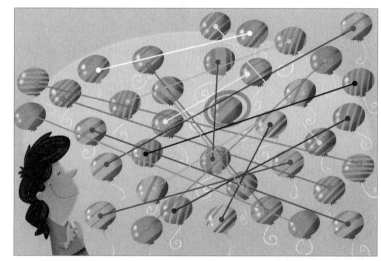

16–17 Look Sharp!

Here are the SH words we found. You may have found others.

shadow	shin
shake	shingles
shampoo	ship
shamrock	shirts
shapes	shoe
shark	shoelace
shave	shop
shaving cream	shopping cart
shawl	shore
sheep	shorts
sheepdog	shoulder
sheet	shout
shells	shovel
shepherd	shower
sheriff	shrimp
Sherlock Holmes	shuffleboard
shield	shutters

18 Moo-ve It Along

Buck: Cowly
Jeannie: Cuddles
Roy: Munch
Sasha: Ferdie
Tex: Moosic

19 Fruit Salad

A					
G	R	A	P	E	S
S	P	E	R	A	G
E	G	S	A	P	R
P	A	R	S	G	E
A	S	G	E	R	P
R	E	P	G	S	A

B					
O	R	A	N	G	E
E	N	G	O	A	R
A	O	N	R	E	G
R	G	E	A	O	N
N	E	O	G	R	A
G	A	R	E	N	O

C					
Q	U	I	N	C	E
C	E	N	U	I	Q
E	N	U	I	Q	C
I	Q	C	E	U	N
U	C	E	Q	N	I
N	I	Q	C	E	U

31

20-21 Pizza Q's

Delivery Dilemma

Pizza Quiz

a. False (It's famous for its thick crust.)
b. True
c. True
d. False (Mozzarella is the most-used pizza cheese.)

Mixed-Up Orders

Peyton: cheese
Isaac: pepperoni
Ethan: Hawaiian

Old World Pizza

Here are some we found:

lane	pile
nail	pin
nap	pine
nation	planet
neat	pot
nine	tail
oil	tea
pail	teal
pan	tile
patio	top

Odd Slice Out

A   B   C   D   E

22-23 Go for the Gold!

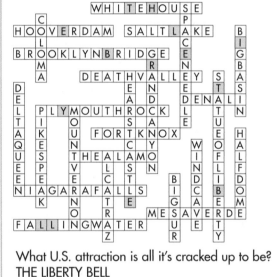

26-27 Vroom, Vroom!

How do dogs like to travel?
BY MUTT-A-CYCLE

28-29 Crisscross the U.S.A.

What U.S. attraction is all it's cracked up to be?
THE LIBERTY BELL

Executive Editor: Mary-Alice Moore
Consulting Editor: Andrew Gutelle
Writer/Editor: Betsy Ochester
Art Director: Marta Ruliffson/Hey Kids!
Production Manager: Margaret Mosomillo

SUSTAINABLE FORESTRY INITIATIVE
Certified Chain of Custody
Promoting Sustainable Forestry
www.sfiprogram.org
SFI-01268